10 Fascinating Facts About Dinosaurs

by Rachel Grack

Content Consultant
Carl Mehling, Senior Scientific Assistant in the Division of Paleontology
American Museum of Natural History

Reading Consultant
Jeanne M. Clidas, Ph.D.
Reading Specialist

Children's Press®
An Imprint of Scholastic Inc.

Table of Contents

Dinosaurs roamed the planet for 165 million years. There were hundreds of species. Then, about 65 million years ago, a huge meteorite or comet hit the Earth. The Age of Dinosaurs came to a sudden end.

Do you want to learn more fascinating facts about dinosaurs? Then read on!

Diplodocus lost A LOT of teeth

Many dinosaurs replaced their teeth every couple of months. *Diplodocus* did so very quickly. It grew new teeth about every 35 days. Not every dino mouth

Diplodocus was a herbivore. It ate plants.

was the same.
For example, plant eaters had different teeth from meat eaters. **Paleontologists** can learn a lot about dinosaurs by studying **fossils** of their teeth. They discover what kind of food dinosaurs ate and how they digested it.

This fossil shows that *Diplodocus* teeth were shaped like pegs.

T. rex had a killer bite

In fact, it had the most powerful bite of any land animal ever known.

T. rex's jaw was 4 feet (1 meter) long!

T. rex could eat 500 pounds (227 kilograms) of meat in only one bite! *Tyrannosaurus rex* means "king of the tyrant lizards." And this dinosaur was one tough customer! It was the top predator of its time.

500 pounds of meat is equal to 620 hamburgers!

DINO FILE

Tyrannosaurus rex

tye-ran-uh-SAWR-us REKS

DIET: This meat eater ate LOTS of other dinosaurs.

LENGTH: up to 40 feet (12 meters)

HEIGHT: up to 40 feet

WEIGHT: 9 tons

Spinosaurus looked like a ship

This dinosaur is the largest known meat eater on land. It had huge webbed spines running down its back. They looked like the sails of a ship. The spines may have made

Spinosaurus's spines were up to 7 feet (2 meters) tall.

Spinosaurus seem bigger to enemies. Some paleontologists believe this was the first swimming dinosaur.

DINO FILE

Spinosaurus
SPY-nuh-SAWR-us

DIET: This meat eater mostly ate seafood.

LENGTH: 40–59 feet (12–18 meters)

WEIGHT: 10–20 tons

Spinosaurus had a long snout and oversized front teeth. Its diet was similar to the diet of present-day crocodiles.

Ankylosaurus was protected with armor

Ankylosaursus uses its tail as a club against T. rex.

T. rex...Spinosaurus... These large meat eaters made the world a dangerous place! Plant eaters needed to protect themselves. *Ankylosaurus* had the best defense. It had bony **armor** in its skin. The armor could stop the sharpest teeth. *Ankylosaurus*'s skin was covered in giant knobs that added even more protection. Some even had armored eyelids.

As seen in this fossil, *Ankylosaurus* had a club at the end of its tail. It was used to defend against predators.

DINO FILE

Ankylosaurus
ang-kuh-loh-SAWR-us

DIET: This plant eater ate low-growing plants

LENGTH:
35 feet (11 meters)

HEIGHT:
4 feet (1 meter)

WIDTH:
6 feet (2 meters)

WEIGHT: 5–6 tons

Triceratops is the most famous horned dino

Triceratops means "three-horned face." These large herbivores made a tasty meal for meat eaters. But *Triceratops* had horns

This is a model of an actual *Triceratops* skeleton.

three horns

that were 3 feet (1 meter) long. It could use its horns to fight off the fiercest predators.

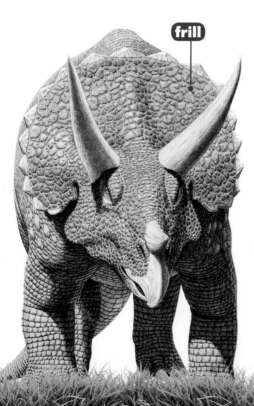

frill

DINO FILE

Triceratops
try-SAIR-uh-tops

DIET: this plant eater ate shrubs

LENGTH: 30 feet (9 meters)

HEIGHT: over 9 feet (3 meters)

WEIGHT: 11 tons

Triceratops had a frill on the back of its head. It may have been a defense against the deadly jaws of a *T. rex*.

Sinosauropteryx had feathers

This is a *Sinosauropteryx* fossil. The dino looks like a long-tailed turkey.

In fact, it was the first dinosaur reported to have feathers. It could not fly, though. Its feathers probably acted like fur

127586

16

to keep it warm. Most scientists believe birds **evolved** from dinosaurs. *Sinosauropteryx* fossils show they might be right!

Scientists were even able to figure out what color feathers this dino had.

Brachiosaurus had a looong neck

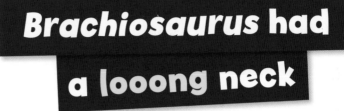

Long-necked dinos like *Brachiosaurus* are called sauropods.

This plant eater was one of the largest dinosaurs. It had to munch a lot of veggies to get full. In fact, *Brachiosaurus* had to eat up to 880 pounds (400 kilograms) of plants every day! This dino's diet included leaves from the tallest trees. Luckily, its super-stretch neck helped *Brachiosaurus* reach the highest branches.

FACT

8

Stegosaurus was
a show-off

This dino's brain was about the size of a walnut.

Stegosaurus was a massive plant eater. It had two rows of huge, pointy plates

20

along its back. Some of the plates were 4 feet (1 meter) tall. They probably protected *Stegosaurus* from predators. They may have also been used the way a peacock uses its feathers— to show off.

A *Stegosaurus's* plates might have changed color when blood rushed into them.

plates

Pachycephalosaurs were boneheads

Pachycephalosaurs might have battled by butting heads.

Some of these dome-headed dinos had skulls up to 9 inches (23 centimeters) thick. The average human skull is just one-quarter of an inch thick. The dome of a pachycephalosaur skull is often the only part of the fossil to be found. That is because it is so thick and hard. In fact, the very first dome discovery was mistaken for a dinosaur kneecap!

Dome-heads got their name from the rounded tops of their skulls.

Hadrosaurs fossils have skin

Hadrosaurs are also known as duckbill dinosaurs. Can you guess why?

Some hadrosaurs remains were discovered with fossil skin covering the skeleton. Skin often rots away when an animal dies. Somehow the hadrosaurs' skin was preserved. Paleontologists know more about hadrosaurs than they do about many other dinosaurs. That is because they have discovered so many fossils. The first nearly full dinosaur fossil ever found was a hadrosaur.

DINO FILE

Hadrosaurs
HAD-ruh-SAWRS

DIET: This plant eater ate low-lying vegetation.

LENGTH: up to 30 feet (9 meters)

HEIGHT: up to 50 feet (15 meters)

WEIGHT: up to 3 tons

Hadrosaurs lived in herds.

Activity
Make a Fossil

Follow these directions to make your very own fossil to study.

You Will Need:

- ✔ sheet of waxed paper
- ✔ modeling clay
- ✔ 2 small paper cups

- ✔ small plastic insect or other object
- ✔ ½ cup plaster of Paris

- ✔ liquid and dry measuring cups
- ✔ ¼ cup water
- ✔ craft stick

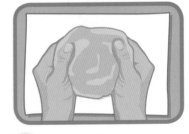

1 Lay out the waxed paper. Place a ball of modeling clay on top and flatten to about ¾-inch thick. Smooth the top.

2 Press the clay into the bottom of one of the cups, with the smooth side up.

3 Carefully press the plastic insect into the clay to make an imprint. Remove the insect.

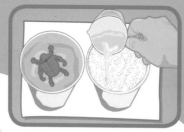

4 Pour the plaster of Paris into the other cup. Add water. Stir with a craft stick until smooth. Let the mixture sit until thickened.

5 Pour the plaster of Paris mixture into the first cup. Let it dry for 24 hours.

6 Tear away the paper cup.

7 Remove your fossil. What does it tell you about the animal from which it was created?

Timeline

The Mesozoic era was the Age of Dinosaurs. This prehistoric era was divided into the Triassic, Jurassic, and Cretaceous periods.

mya: million years ago

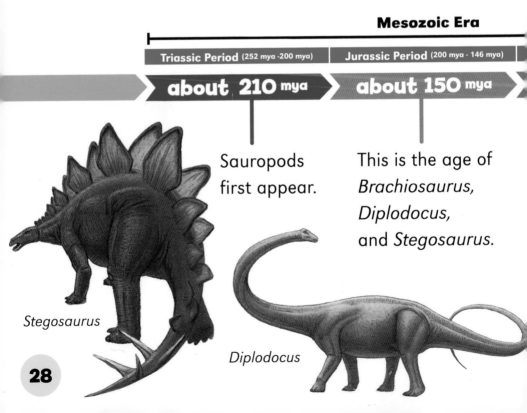

Triceratops

Mesozoic Era

Triassic Period (252 mya -200 mya)	Jurassic Period (200 mya - 146 mya)
about 210 mya	**about 150 mya**

Sauropods first appear.

This is the age of *Brachiosaurus, Diplodocus,* and *Stegosaurus.*

Stegosaurus

Diplodocus

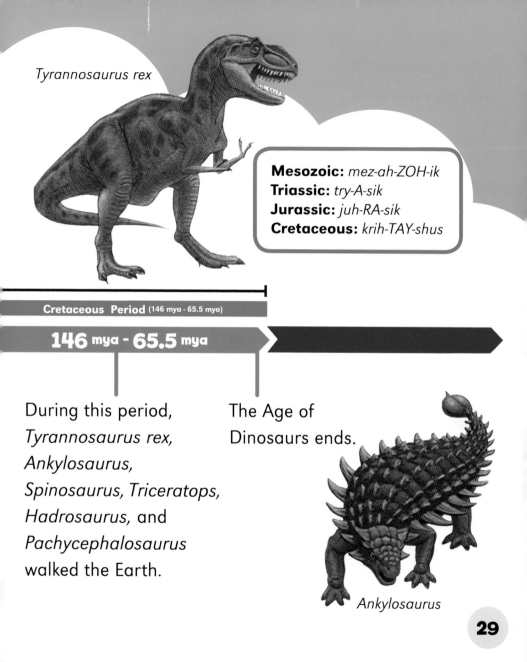

Tyrannosaurus rex

Mesozoic: *mez-ah-ZOH-ik*
Triassic: *try-A-sik*
Jurassic: *juh-RA-sik*
Cretaceous: *krih-TAY-shus*

Cretaceous Period (146 mya - 65.5 mya)

146 mya **- 65.5** mya

During this period, *Tyrannosaurus rex, Ankylosaurus, Spinosaurus, Triceratops, Hadrosaurus,* and *Pachycephalosaurus* walked the Earth.

The Age of Dinosaurs ends.

Ankylosaurus

Glossary

armor (AHR-mur): protective scales, spines, or shells that cover some animals and plants

evolved (ih-VAHLVD): changed slowly and naturally over time

fossils (FAH-suhls): bones, shells, or other traces of an animal or a plant from millions of years ago

paleontologists (pay-lee-uhn-TAH-luh-jists): scientists who study fossils

Index

About the Author

Rachel Grack has been writing children's nonfiction since 2001. She lives on a farm in Casa Grande, Arizona. Her favorite pastimes are enjoying her family and her barnyard of animals. She has goats, cats, a horse named Lady, and some dino descendants—also known as chickens! Rachel dedicates this book to her grandson Keaton: May your imagination grow so fierce it roars!

Facts for Now

Visit this Scholastic Web site for
more information on dinosaurs:

www.factsfornow.scholastic.com

Enter the keyword **Dinosaurs**

Library of Congress Cataloging-in-Publication Data

Names: Koestler-Grack, Rachel A., 1973- author.
Title: 10 fascinating facts about dinosaurs/by Rachel Grack.
Other titles: Ten fascinating facts about dinosaurs
Description: New York, NY: Children's Press, an imprint of Scholastic Inc.,
[2017] | Series: Rookie star fact finder | Includes index.
Identifiers: LCCN 2016030338| ISBN 9780531222607 (library binding) | ISBN 9780531226766 (pbk.)
Subjects: LCSH: Dinosaurs—Juvenile literature.
Classification: LCC QE861.5 .K64 2017 | DDC 567.9—dc23
LC record available at https://lccn.loc.gov/2016030338

Produced by Spooky Cheetah Press
Design by Judith Christ-Lafond

© 2017 by Scholastic Inc.

Photographs ©: cover: Mark Stevenson/Media Bakery; cover background, back cover background: stock09/Shutterstock, Inc.; back cover: Friedrich Saurer/Alamy Images; 2 top: Leonello Calvetti/Getty Images; 2-3 grass: Anan Kaewkhammul/Shutterstock, Inc.; 2-3 dino: Elenarts/Fotolia; 4-5 background: Larry Geddis/Alamy Images; 5 top left: Roger Harris/Science Photo Library/Getty Images; 5 top right: Mr1805/Dreamstime; 5 center right: Stocktrek Images, Inc/Alamy Images; 5 bottom right: Elenarts/Fotolia; 5 girl: Luis Louro/Dreamstime; 6 tree: Nopporn0510/Dreamstime; 6 main: Catmando/Fotolia; 7 dino size comp illustrations and throughout: Keith Plechaty; 7 bottom: Kent Dannen/Getty Images; 8: Elena Duvernay/Stocktrek Images/Getty Images; 9 bottom: Drozhzhina Elena/Shutterstock, Inc.; 10: The Washington Post/Getty Images; 10 bottom left, 11 bottom: Mohamad Haghani/Stocktrek Images/Getty Images; 12: Kurt Miller/Stocktrek Images/Getty Images; 13 bottom: Andy Crawford/Dorling Kindersley; 14-15 grass: Anan Kaewkhammul/Shutterstock, Inc.; 14 skeleton: starmaro/Shutterstock, Inc.; 15 dino: Dorling Kindersley/Getty Images; 16 left: Bernard Weil/Getty Images; 16-17 background: yanikap/Shutterstock, Inc.; 16-17 dino: Nobumichi Tamura/Stocktrek Images/Getty Images; 18-19 bottom: Roger Harris/Science Photo Library/Getty Images; 20 center left: gosphotodesign/Fotolia; 20 bottom: Elenarts/Fotolia; 21 bottom: Friedrich Saurer/Alamy Images; 22: amberstock/Alamy Images; 23 bottom: Jim Lane/Alamy Images; 24: PhotoStock-Israel/Alamy Images; 25 bottom: Mr1805/Dreamstime; 26-27 illustrations: Keith Plechaty; 26-27 craft kids: Christopher Futcher/iStockphoto; 28-29 all dinos: Richard Courtney; 30 top: Kurt Miller/Stocktrek Images/Getty Images; 30 center top: Elenarts/Fotolia; 30 center bottom: Andy Crawford/Getty Images; 30 bottom: microgen/Getty Images.